Capture their moments
Share their stories.

Let Me Take Y'all Back

by Yasmine Brown

iiPUBLISHING

Let Me Take Y'all Back
Copyright © 2021 by Yasmine Brown

Copyright notice
All rights reserved. No part of this book may be reproduced in any form or by any electronic or mechanical means, including information storage and retrieval systems, without permission in writing from the author or publisher, except for the use of brief quotations in a book review.

Cover design by tonii

ISBN: 978-1-7362167-2-9

Printed in the United States of America

iiPUBLISHING

New York, NY
www.toniiinc.com

Table of Contents

stolen bike	*2*
brownstone kiss	*4*
menstruation	*6*
virginity	*8*
the girls room	*10*
mockery	*12*
depression	*14*
break through	*16*
mental health check	*18*
parental fear	*20*
the movie	*22*
outside the norm	*24*
coffee in the morning	*26*
body language	*28*
shopping right?	*30*
learning soul ties	*32*
death of an old lover	*34*
the stage	*36*
being star struck	*38*
real friendship	*40*
coming out	*42*
making history	*44*
protest	*46*
getting caught	*48*
separation	*50*
older experience	*52*
same guy	*54*
pulling up	*56*
business and pleasure	*58*
at peace	*60*

"

Let Me Take Y'all Back
tells the tales of different individuals' life experience in a raw and authentic approach. You will be taken on a journey through each unique story that I was blessed to hear and given permission to write. This is their truths. This is their voice pushed out of my pen. I want every reader to know "you are not alone." We may have different paths and stories, but it is in the sharing of our truths that we realize our common thread as people. Let our stories connect us.

"Woke up the next morning, niggas had stole my bike"

Fifty, if I didn't feel anything else you said
I definitely felt that line
I know it seems childish
But it's a grudge I can't leave behind
Here I am gassed up
Riding freely as if I just bought a new car
Head with the stars
Not realizing you were plotting on me all along
After that moment that's where the child went wrong
You see, now the world doesn't look like
Fluffs and candy
More like, it seems pretty crappy
The rules of the streets were learned quickly
You got to take or be the one taken
Trust no one and sleep with one eye open
I didn't want to be this cold
But the hood makes it so simple
My sadness as a kid went from woe is me to

You know how that shit go.

They say the best love stories start off as friends
Well this one doesn't quite have love at the end
He was older, but not R.Kelly vibes
Something like the next grade up
My buddy, more like a brother
He wasn't that fine
But personality can overpower looks
Well for some people
But this feature I couldn't overlook
Just a regular after-school day
If you was in, then, you'd kick it at Ben's brownstone
& I was cooler than cool
Today my bro was different
He had a weird look in his eyes
The vibe was off but it'll get weirder after this line
He leaned in and kissed me
His puckers took up half of my face
I don't know what was worse
The smell of slob or that my first kiss was of distaste
You wait for this moment to come
& for it to be romantic and sunny
But mine was like kissing a frog,
No romance just comedy
So in the end my lesson learned
Was to never accept a kiss from a friend.

Brownstone Kiss

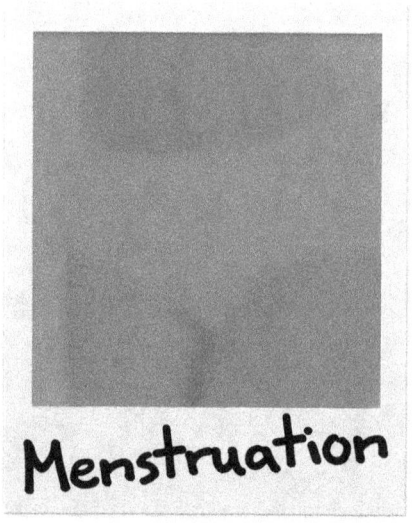

Who's punching bag am I?
Tell eve I need a meeting with her
I don't understand why I'm paying for her
Rotten apple mistakes
I'd prefer red wine in my cup, not in my pants
God, please hear me out
I think we get it
Please stop making me pay for
The next girl's mistakes.

He was the new boy and I was just that girl
I didn't know much
But I knew there was something there
& you felt it too
I thought we'd be together forever
At twelve what the hell was I thinking?
But this was at a time
I had no business singing 'bump and grind'
So who could blame me?
Young and dumb
Barely knowing anything about virginity
But I knew it could be lost
He was the one that found it
& took my innocence too
That sour patch turned sour real fast
I found out people leave
Once they get what they want from you.

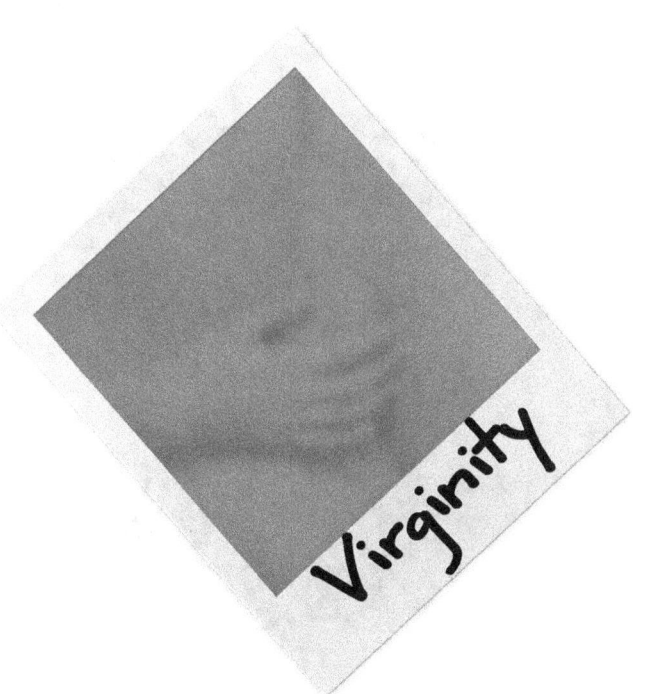

The Girls Room

Paradise of Strangers,
Stumbling into the bathroom
With a full bladder
& cup filled,
Searching for an empty mirror,
Silly laughter,
Sexual compliments,
Same sex kissing,
Drunken dancing and tequila breath,
Life story short term memory gossip,
Re-applying mascara and lipstick,
Bonding over femininity,
Entering a world only women understand,
Sharing insecurities,
Embracing each other's features,
Enjoying each other's company,
Brief universal transition,
But once you stumble out...*poof*...
Hang overs and memory loss,
Blurry thoughts but you just remember
Those nice girls in the bathroom,
No name, no face,
Just nice girls.

They called me out of my name
My heart ripped out of my chest
While they were laughing
I was bleeding
Your tears of joy cost me knives plunged in my back
Your giggles caused me wounds that won't heal
You've watched me cry over heart ache
& then joined the list
I lost the second love of my life
Friendship.

Mockery

I want to die
I've thought of every way to do it
I've already popped a perc
A few more should do it
Maybe a razor and slice each arm...yeah, that'll do
Drive as fast as I can
& flip the car over... yeah, that's a good one too
Don't worry this isn't a suicide note
But more of a cry for help
I'd try to attempt these things
But I can't move
So my heart will just have to stop itself
I'm trying to see this light at the end of the tunnel
It isn't going well, I feel.
So this is my last chance at calling for help.
Can you help me heal?

A couple of days ago,
If you'd looked up the definition of "rock bottom,"
You'd see me
I could eat,
Function,
Or do anything that involved moving my feet
A few days ago,
I would've took my life
& no one would've known
But it wasn't until I had a conversation with my bro
He said he had the same thoughts as me
Without me saying a word
I advised that life without him would be absurd
"Why the hell would you do that?"
(Look at me being hypocritical)
I had the same feelings of being selfish too
Ending my life and leaving you

"Promise me this:

Have a talk with someone
When life gets this dark
Your life ending
Will cause someone else's to fall apart."

BreakThrough

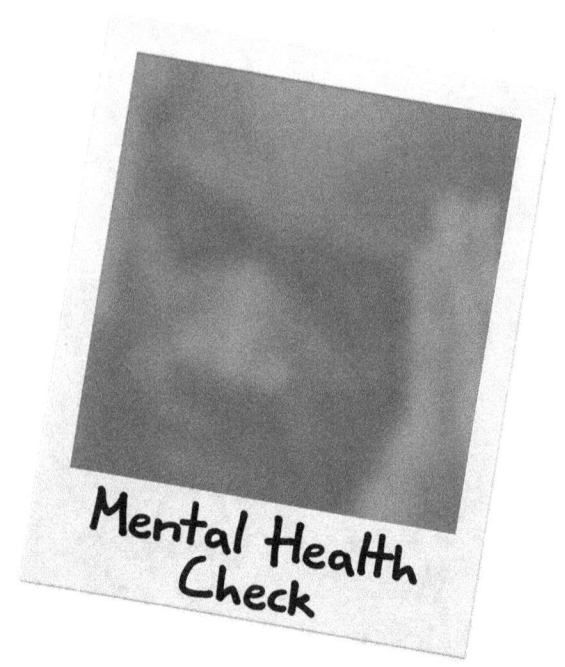

Mental Health Check

As a black person, I have to be strong
As a man, I have to be powerful
As a black man, I have to be both
Out of the womb, I have to take this oath
Yet, I am ashamed
Because I was never taugh that
Focusing on mental health is apart of being woke
Scared on the inside that if I spoke out
They'll cut my throat
Instilled in my mind to hang myself
With the imaginary rope
That was given by society
So today I will try the first steps to sobriety
Admit the problem at hand
Let everyone know in this battle of silence...
I take a stand
That way, I am in the right state of mind
To be a better man
That way, I can teach others and speak up
On being a black man.

I finally stood up to the big bad wolf
Yes, even the toughest people have fears too
But I would have rather been sliced by Jason
Than to face you
So instead, I put on this happy face
Pretended to go along and laugh at your jokes
Like you didn't do me wrong
I wasn't scared of a fist fight...we've done that before
I was more terrified
That I wouldn't get what I asked for
Just a little but more of your time
I'm screaming for it and losing my mind
So, when I finally told you how I felt
I had to laugh because you proved me right
Now how do I heal?
This heartbreak is worse than
Any lover or friend can do
But imma be alright
& raise my kids better than you could ever do.

Parental Fear

The Movie

You see, he was with his girl and I was with my guy
& we were both just an audience to a movie
He was coming out of the bathroom
& we locked eyes, while I was waiting to get popcorn
He licked his lips
I twirled my curls
He smirked and I melted
"Miss, here's your popcorn"
I looked back to finish our convo
Only to find he disappeared
After the lights come on
& the credits filled the screen
Under his leather jacket arm I looked over
& to my surprise it's you behind that girl
We conversed again for about five more minutes
Only to go back to our lives
You see, he wasn't mine and I wasn't his
Timing wasn't on our side but...
Oh, what a great movie.

He didn't approach her like the rest
Never even asked for her number at first
His pants didn't hang below his waist
All his cards were owned by him
No record, no drugs, no scams
Just him
He didn't speak much
But spoke enough
His eyes were like a puzzle
It felt like he was staring into my soul
His kisses were chocolate
His hands were cotton
He was gentle
Peace in a room full of noise
Love in a world full of hate
He was different.

Outside the Norm

Coffee in the Morning

Stretching,
Grasping a fist full of covers
She struts freely into the kitchen
Gazing at him drinking his coffee
Biting her lip and loudly giggling in the doorway
He smirks, but doesn't look back
She walks and slowly plops herself onto the counter
He watches her breast bounce
& outlines her curves with his eyes
She smiles and stares at her dangling feet
She slowly picks up her head
Their eyes fill the room with chatter
He gestures his glass to her
As she reaches for the glass he whispers,

What's your name beautiful?

He spoke to me so sweet
His words knocked me off my feet
& picked me back up with the same sentence
The way he looked at me
As if I was a star
His eyes spoke a foreign language
They danced all over my body
I was like a deer in headlights
Without even saying it, I knew his thoughts
This was like an open book test
He put his head in my lap
I ran my fingers through his beard
He closed his eyes and I whispered,

I love you too.

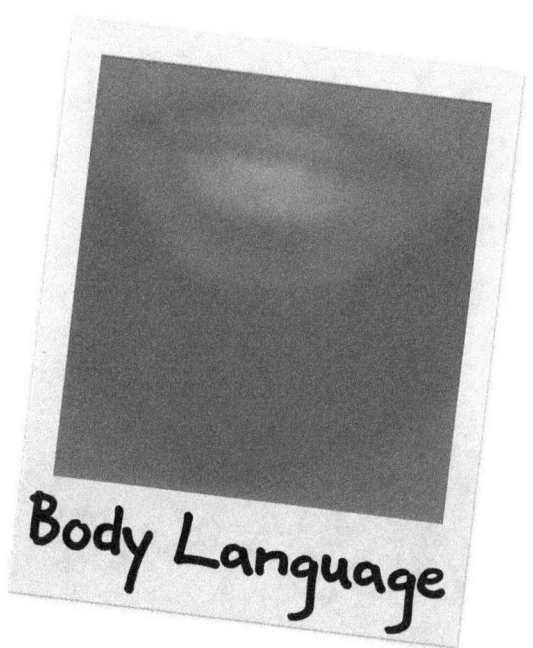

Body Language

After a while, all of these shopping aisles look the same
Like a bar, you start to get regulars
& everyone begins to know your name
So eventually it goes to your head
(You know that hood fame)
It was a regular night of putting throwbacks away
I was working two jobs, so it was a long ass day
The store was ordinary just full of regulars
But wait, I spot this giant that isn't too familiar
He caught my eye when he passed by
Then, I saw him again in aisle 6
Then, his face kept appearing around and I'm thinking,
"Ok, obviously he wants more than pancake mix"
I turned and stared in those hazel pretty eyes
Almost distracted me from the question I had in mind,
"Are you following me?"
"No, do you want me to?"
He replied.
A sassy filled "no" fluttered from my lips
But he saw through my tough shell
& knew that was a lie
He said, "alright then"
So I turned and walked away
I guess he couldn't let me go that easy
Because he then asked me for my name.

Every soul you encounter teaches you

There was my first soul
My very first soul
My forbidden fruit
You see, I was eve and I thought he was Adam but...
He turned out to be the serpent
Then, I encountered souls that were smooth and secret,
The closet souls
The *I wasn't hiding you from the world,*
I was hiding the world from you souls
The *I'm not good enough for your brand*
but good for your bed souls
Then, came another,
The double soul
The *I love you but fuck you* soul
The *no one will ever wife you but me* soul
The toxic soul

But through the soul searching and pain
I finally found a sweet soul,
A pure soul
The *no he isn't perfect*
but his ties perfectly with mine soul
The kind soul
The *fights my inner demons and brings me peace* soul
I found the *light to my darkest moments* soul
The *make me whole* soul
The soul that taught me this:

Be careful who you tie yourself to
Because souls follow you wherever you go,
Like light or shadows
So, make sure you know the difference.

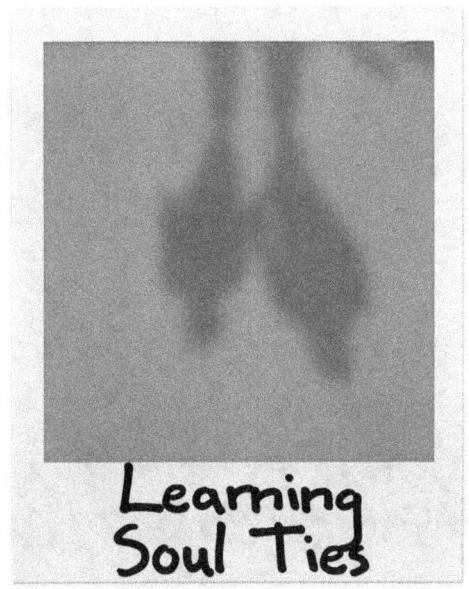

Learning Soul Ties

We had that *hood* love
I mean that *good hood* love
That *drinking forties and wearing pelle coats* love
Stealing cars and playing with guns for a joke love
Abusive in private but that never made it to a post love
Conditional disguised in unconditional clothing love
I love you but pride won't let me stay with you love
We said things we didn't mean, love
Made decisions that weren't clean, love
Made apologies that were in vain, love
We held on to grudges and bottled up our pain, love
But all these words will be for nothing now, love
I'm sorry if you can't come around, love
I forgive you now, love
I hope you forgive me too
For taking so long to apologize to you, love
You were many things and some better left unsaid, love
So goodbye for now, love
I hope you found peace where you rest, love

All the best,
Love

Everyone looks like a bag of popcorn
I'm scared to reach my hand towards that dark bag
My mouth moves but nothing flows
I take two steps back
As my eyes search for the exit
Your spotlight catches my peripheral vision
Dazed in your aura I stand there
Eyes closed...
I picture how your hands feel exploring my body
As I stand
You massage my words out of my mouth
With your tongue
You sway my body and guide my hips to the rhythm
As I pause waiting for you to just give me your name
The popcorn people start popping
Your mirage disappears, as I open my eyes
& you appear back into my peripheral
Thank you for getting me through the time.

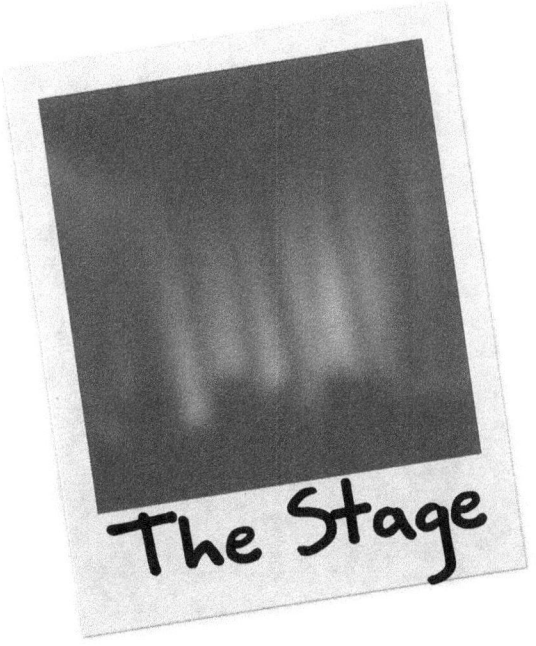
The Stage

The Pickup

Excuse me...
Pops tripping he said I gotta come over here
& ask for my heart back
I know right?
Who does he think he is, telling me I got it bad?
I don't usually do this often,
But your beauty got me thinking
You'd be the best thing I'll ever have

& my mom's tripping too
She said you're too much in my dome
She don't even know
I haven't gotten into how I wanna give you both domes
I know that might've flew over your head...
I'm praying it did

I don't want to come on too hard
I know I'm rambling
But I'm thinking about all the right things to say to you
Well, at this point...*fuck it*,
Imma be a man and let you know
I'm tryna get to know you.

She said *"will you pray with me?"*
Five words that calmed my spirit
After years of mistreatment
She knew I wasn't mentally there
So, instead of kicking me down like the rest
She asked me to kneel
Join with her and leave it at the side of the bed
Because when two gather in his name,
You are not calling him in vain
Your worries and troubles are now dead
She thought of me enough to
Spiritually cuff us together
No, we aren't disciples
But I knew she wasn't Peter and she realized
I was surrounded by Judas
So instead of nailing me, she comforted
Like a prophet, she help me with this epiphany
Separating the ties with these entities
Became easier for me
The grass now appears green
Instead of sorrow and hatred
A friend came and lifted my spirits
& one line contributed to my perseverance:
Will you pray with me?

Coming Out

In the beginning
We are taught that Adam and Eve is the order
So anything out of that is considered a disorder
If I speak up about it, I may be tortured
Yes, we have parades
But that doesn't stop our genre from becoming horror
So you can understand
It wasn't easy coming out to my mother
But I did it
I prayed in this world for her to remain my rock
She'll be shocked
But after, she will take a step back to realize
Before anything, I am her son
This isn't a feeling that can be undone
The last thing i need is for my family to run
What I need is for you to accept my truth

I was so relieved that my prayers came true
As she said to me,
"I accept you".

Out of 650 people I was chosen
In this moment I valued favor
Not from man but from God
Not from me being the right skin
But for the knowledge within my noggin
I can lay down those moments
For a moment of feeling defeated
All of the sleepless nights were finally for a reason
I can step in the courts
& make a difference when things get heated
Who knew that me helping my people
Would start by convincing judges to listen?
I am touched that I can now be a voice of reason
Show that you can make a difference in a system
That isn't created to let blacks win
To my fellow people, this is only the beginning.

Making History

Today, I fought for what's right
Cops surrounded the site
Night sticks and guns were prepared to go off
Yet, we as protesters only used our mouths
Yellow tape was the symbol of 'not to cross the line'
&, sadly, if someone tripped and ripped it
We all would've died
Black men and women in blue suits
Put on the front lines
While their white coworkers hid behind
Emotions of fear ran inside
Yet, I ate that up and stood with pride
In this moment, I didn't care if I died
If that's what it took for my people to get their rights
If the yellow border broke and I had to fight
My bloody smile would've gleamed
Brighter than any lights
I would've slept well with however it went tonight
Because either way the future is changing
For my kids to have more rights
I marched
For my black husband to come back to me each night
I marched
So I don't have to have anxiety attacks
When my brother is out all night
I marched
Because I want being black to be legalized foresight
Sadly, many of you may read this
& think this a piece from the 60's
I want all generations to know
Baby, this day took place within 2020.

I told this nigga to have my money
& every convo he ends up short
But, so is my temper
He thinks I'm a joke, so the rules are simple
I'm nothing to fuck with
We running up, no masks as an example
I'm taking everything as collateral
& if the nigga squint wrong,
He's getting popped like a pimple
We pulled up and no surprise he was scared as fuck
We checked his pockets, no luck
So my right hand put the glock to his head
But before he struck
I told him until he has my money
We'll ride off in his G-wagon truck
The nerve of this nigga not paying what he owes
But...I fucked up
Not thinking he wouldn't snitch on his foe
"Somebody call my girl"
I looked up from the concrete
My daughter staring into my eyes from a far
Next time, I'll remember to lay low in a stolen car.

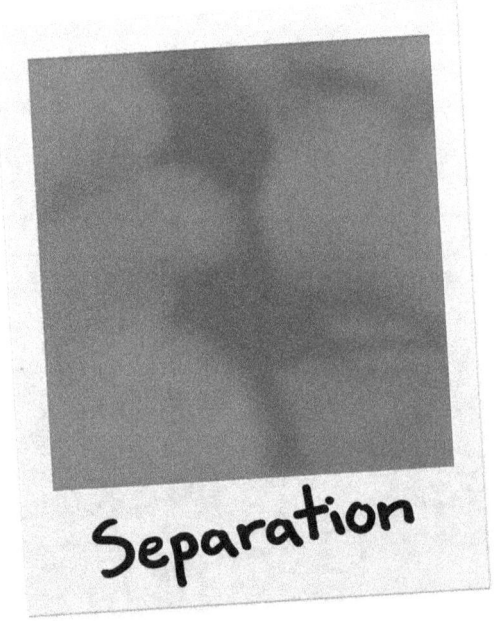

Separation

She was perfection
Brown skin complexion
Her thickness made me feel blessed and
For her, I cooked, cleaned,
Shoot, I'd even fold her dresses
Why? Because she was my blessing
& my rib...so without her, a piece of me is missing
Yet, I should've known she was no good
When my gestures gave her no meaning
The kisses turned into dodges
I'm prayed but it felt like I had no progress
I don't know why she won't look at me the same
Does she not want to be monogamous?
What's he got that I don't?
This is crazy
I went through her phone to see which body bag to use
How hefty?
How could she cheat on me with this dude?
I barked on her crazy
Then, my heart dropped to my gut
When she told me, he's a lady
& just like that
She's now a bitch
The no good ones, I should've known would switch
I could get passed you cheating with someone
With more of an inch
But instead you'd rather bump fish
I couldn't make you moan, so you'd rather a girl
That looks like me but sits when she has to piss
I'm crushed
But I care more about our kids
Mommy and daddy are no more
It's mommy and mommy now
With all due respect,
I love you, but you gotta get out.

It's New Years, but it's the same party every year
My sisters friends turn up
& because it's at our house I'm an honorary guest
But this night was different
A girl noticed me differently from the rest
Her face wasn't familiar
She lured me upstairs
While everyone was too drunk to care
She made me feel like a man
& getting off wasn't in tonight's plans
But neither was this next line
Seeing my sister come in
As if, shawty committed a crime ,
Busting heads different from the way shawty did mine
Watching tears flow from my mom and my sister
On our way to the precinct
I was too blind to face this
But I woke up, after they told me
I have to do a rape kit.

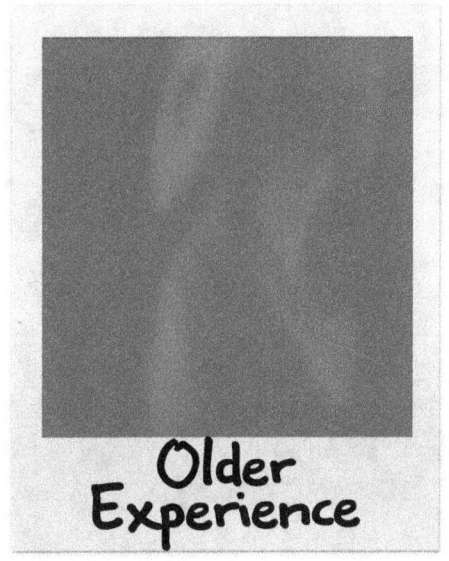

Older Experience

So there's this guy I know
But you may know a different side
I'm sure he gave everyone a different vibe
He caused some to laugh and some to cry
His death was ruled out as a homicide
But it can be argued because the streets are suicide
No matter how much you try to do right
Your past catches up to you
Our minds still try to wrap our brains around
Who killed you
The streets are to blame
I was stunned to know there's more people like him
& we're all just told to *charge it to the game.*

My mom is in the hospital
That's what I kept chanting not believing what I see
Out of 365 days
You decide when my mom is sick to cheat on me
With a girl that isn't even a percentage of me
She can try all her life but she'd never finish loading
I'm crying my eyes out
& this is why my calls, you're ignoring
While I'm concerned about my mothers life
You're in here moaning
& here you are in my face dumb and surprised
After trashing your apartment, before I leave
Let me end this TV with my doc martins
You're lucky I didn't leave you and that girl
Lifeless on the carpet.

Pulling Up

& in this moment I knew I messed up
I know I said strictly business
But this vibe makes me wanna get unprofessional
With this liquor going and words slurring
I wanna get more personal
I told my lover I wouldn't take it this far
But I'd go the extra mile for you
In mid sentence,
I'm ready to press my lips up against you
See, the physical attraction didn't catch my attention
But your mind is what met my eye
I'm tryna unlock my phone to catch an Uber
But you got me mesmerized
Like damn baby!
Who taught you to say everything I wanted to hear?
I wonder is the cheaters van near
Because I'm about to get in trouble
With all these feelings I have inside
I know I told you I have someone
But they're the last thing on my mind
They probably would kill me, if they heard that last line
But sadly I don't give a damn
We've only met up a few times for work
But yet here I am falling head over heels
I'll probably regret this in the morning
But let's go get a room
So you can come give me some more thrills.

Cocaine sands so rich someone would try to sniff it
Fifty shades of blue
Vibrantly moving towards me
Sweat glistening kissing my body as it trickles down
The gorgeous sun smiling at me as I close my eyes
& exhale it all in
The voice of the water giving loud whispers
The smirk of loneliness providing contentment
I'm alive
I am one.

the content of this book is based on true stories from real conversations.

Afterword

Thank you for reading and rocking with me until the end of the book! It is my hope that you enjoyed this first poetry collection in the *Let Me Take Y'all Back* series. The purpose of this series is to capture people's moments in life, like a polaroid picture. Using poetry, I highlighted the fundamental lessons found in conversations that I believe has the ability to save a life or at least, inspire one. I want people to know and understand that there is power in your individual stories, moments, and experiences, but it cannot be released unless it is shared with others. I hope you found a lesson within a poem written, hope with these words expressed, and/or inspiration from one or all of the stories I shared.

Stayed tuned for part two.

Yasmine Brown

Yasmine Brown is an author, poet, and spoken word artist from Long Island, NY, who started writing short stories in fifth grade, and found her passion for poetry shortly after in middle school. Over the years, she has perfected her craft and brought her words to life by performing spoken word at various open mics in New York and with the publishing of her first poetry collection entitled, "Property Of You" in 2020. Her work is not only for her own therapy, but for the betterment of others. She uses the world around her to inspire her poems, as her surroundings and the people in it become muses in the creative process that she refers to as 'Pushing Her Pen.' This approach makes her work and style unique, as allows herself to be just a pen capturing the voices of her inspiration.

If you enjoyed her work, you should follow her social media pages and order a copy of her first collection at the following link:

https://linktr.ee/yas_daplug.

www.ingramcontent.com/pod-product-compliance
Lightning Source LLC
Chambersburg PA
CBHW062152100526
44589CB00014B/1802